The
WOUNDED
Child

The
WOUNDED
Child

A Real-Life Story of Healing and Hope

Ariel Delgado

Te Wounded Child

Copyright © 2021 by Ariel Delgado

ISBN-13: 978-1736564288

Content Editor: Dylan Johnson

Edited by Mackenzie Richardson

Cover design: Scott Soliz

Cover Image: Cooper Ross

Printed in the United States of America

DEDICATION

I dedicate this book to the following people:
To My Precious Daughters:
Angelina Delgado
Juliana Delgado

To My Mom:
Carmen Gladis Acevedo Noda

To My Dad:
Gregorio René Delgado Fernández

To My Siblings:
Estela Delgado, Fabio Delgado, Diego Delgado

To All the Delgado female and male descendants to come.

To My Friends and mentors:
Jose Ruiz (Tito)
Milton Sellanes
Gabriel Guevara (Polaco)
Chris Beal
Trey Dixon
Greg Gunn
Ray Sanders
Randy Allsbury
Brian and Marla Hill
Chris Ladyga
Juan Pablo Suárez
Juan Contreras

Table of Contents

FOREWORD

I had no idea.

Have you ever met someone only to find out later that they were someone famous or had an incredible story? You had been with them for a while but had no idea who they were or what they had gone through? Such is my experience with Ariel Delgado. I had no idea about this man other than the fact that we shared many interests and friends.

I knew him to be a charming, inspiring and super friendly man that happened to also serve one of my clients. While I spent my day coaching leaders in the company, helping them navigate the challenges of their professional and personal lives, Ariel spent his time building relationships with all the employees as their corporate chaplain. He was known for checking in on them to make sure everything was going okay in their lives. I had no idea that he was a former top corporate executive with a leading national company, traveled the world as an international speaker and lived a life that could have easily been a Hollywood suspense thriller. I simply had no idea!

Between meetings with our shared client, we would often have casual conversations. Those conversations ultimately led to a deep and meaningful friendship; unlike few I have ever known before. It was through this friendship that our stories unfolded.

We were amazed to discover how similar our backgrounds were despite having grown up in different parts of the world. He on a farm in South America while I grew up in a rural North American small town. We had faced different challenges and different issues, but one thing connected us; brokenness, hurt and abuse at the hands of others. Our childhoods had brought plenty of trauma but through the challenges we faced, we had both found hope in knowing Jesus.

Everyone has a story. Ariel's story is both tragic and triumphant. It took him years to find the courage to share his story. I'm glad he did. Through this book, Ariel takes readers with him into the darker side of his life. It is as though we are with him, at his side, experiencing every painstaking blow.

But then there is hope! We find ourselves cheering him on as he discovers the key to overcoming incredible adversity. We are inspired by his courage and willingness to be so honest, vulnerable and real. His story causes us to recognize our own brokenness and pain as we too consider the key to prevailing in all that life has thrown our way. Ariel may have been a victim, but he has turned what was intended for evil into something incredibly good!

What a gift Ariel Delgado is to the world. His story is

destined to inspire and bring hope to all that have ever spoken of another, "I had no idea!"

Ray Sanders

Cofounder of Coaching Leaders, Edify Leaders and

a friend like a brother to the one and only, Ariel Delgado!

CHAPTER 1

Cast all your anxiety on him because he cares for you.

1Peter 5:7 (NIV)

Where Wounds Begin

Children recognize dysfunction at a young age. Children learn from their father at a young age.

When my sister, Estela, and I were very young, we realized that our family wasn't normal. In fact, we were dysfunctional. It didn't take long for me to start learning some bad habits from my family. But that didn't mean my family was all bad.

I come from Uruguay, a small, beautiful South American country between Argentina and Brazil. My childhood may have been difficult at times, but I'm very proud of my heritage, and Uruguay will always be close to my heart. It is an amazing country. I would love to see revival and restoration there.

My father was a prime example of a man in Uruguay. He was a tough, hard-working man, always doing everything within his power to provide for his family. For example, when I was ten, my mom was in the hospital due to pregnancy complications. My father worked on a farm every day to provide for our family, and then took a bus to the city every weekend to be with my mom. I did my part by working with him at the farm and cooking and cleaning daily.

About one month before my mom gave birth to my twin brothers, Fabio and Diego, hardship struck our family. My father lost his farm job and we moved to a little house a couple of miles away from Libertad, the largest city in the area. The house didn't have running water or heat. My sister and I would have to make multiple trips a week to our aunt's house and draw water from a well, before carrying the 10-gallon bucket back home. It took a lot for two little kids to not trip and fall while carrying the massive bucket.

The load wasn't any lighter when it came to heat. We had a small wood burning stove and we had to use whatever scraps we could find to start even a small fire. Since that was our only source of heat, we often had to take cold showers in the middle of frigid winters. How did we keep warm at night? The answer, bricks. I remember rushing to my room after yanking the brick out of the fire. I shifted it from a towel to an old sweater. Then, I waited. After ten or fifteen minutes, I removed the brick and wrapped my little body in the warm sweater. I hoped the heat would hold for the night. Once the fire produced a fair amount of heat, the house would be filled with smoke because our chimney didn't work well. Neither condition was great.

This was normal life for my sister and me. We knew it was bad, but we didn't know how bad it truly was. However, my parents did know and they even gave up meals so that my sister and I could eat. My dad did everything that he could for the family that he loved dearly.

He had a common philosophy among men in my home country. *A real man is always strong. He never shows weakness. If you show weakness, you're no man.*

My dad had to be a man, but he still needed a way to relieve the stress, so he turned to drinking. He would go to a bar with his friends in a little neighboring town and would take me with him. For the first several months, we both loved it. I sat on a barstool sipping a non-alcoholic drink, while my dad drank some alcoholic beverages and laughed with his friends. I just watched and listened, soaking in lessons on what it meant to be a real man.

"A real man protects and provides for his family."

Not all of these lessons were bad.

"A real man takes what he wants and gives others what they deserve."

Some were.

"A real man knows how to get a woman into his bed."

Some were terrible.

It didn't take long for the fun to end. Soon, my dad stopped acting like himself at the bar. He stumbled around, barely making it out the door. The weight of my superhero dad nearly crushed my ten-year-old body as I tried to guide him through the dark, empty streets.

I started to see our dysfunction more clearly. Every day,

it broke my heart a little more than the day before.

My sister and I wanted a normal family who stayed together and loved each other. Yes, we did love each other, but working in fields after school every day to help chip in didn't seem "normal". Leaning over and working the ground didn't feel like a kid's job.

I was now eleven years old and all the stories of manhood at the bar coursed through my brain day after day. I felt like it was time for me to become a man. I needed to follow in my father's footsteps.

I grew up being very protective of my sister as she worked around other guys. If they tried anything with her, I would step up and give them what they deserve. I also started making older friends, growing close to one young man in particular. We talked about every topic you could think of and I really looked up to him. He was older, so he could help me become a man, right? Little did I know that this friendship would take a life-shattering turn.

Lessons Learned

If you can't already tell, I have some wounds in my life. Wounds aren't just caused by physical damage. Trauma can cause a wound in our heart, not just on our skin. Most of the deepest wounds came from my childhood. I'll discuss my most significant wound in the next chapter, but before I get ahead of myself, I need you to know that we all have wounds. They are very distinct from one person to another and they manifest themselves in very different forms, but we all have them.

With that in mind, I want to start by talking about the earliest wounds that all of us experience: Wounds inflicted by our parents. That may already resonate with some of you, but others may be thinking, "Huh? I had awesome parents!" I'm not trying to take away from that. In the book *Wild at Heart*, Author, John Eldridge claims that every person is wounded by their parents somehow.

Think about it: If we are believers in Jesus, we know that every person has sinned, wronging God and others through the thoughts of our minds, attitudes of our hearts, and actions. Every human being, except for Jesus, has been separated from a relationship with our perfect God because of these sins and the ultimate punishment for sin is death and not being able to spend eternity with our Father in Heaven. Only Jesus' death on the cross takes that punishment. Only Him coming back to life three days later offers us a permanent hope of salvation from sin and death, allowing us to have a restored relationship with God now and forever.

Think about that in terms of our parents: Even the best parent has sinned, and even if they've trusted in Jesus, they're still imperfect until they are with God forever. Sometimes, they wound us without realizing it.

My story is a good example. The first wound that my father inflicted on me was his heavy drinking. Hanging out in the bar with him and carrying him home drunk molded my view of manhood and of fatherhood. The second wound, which came later, was when my parents separated. Every kid wants a happy, loving family, but that was ripped from me and my parents didn't even comprehend how much it hurt their children.

Now, I want you to picture these wounds as rocks in a backpack. Wounds don't have to be some big, heartbreaking scene out of a movie, either. Sometimes, a wound can be something as simple as a parent saying to you "You can't do anything right."

Those words and actions stick with us. We can't just blame our parents, either. We put some of our own wounds in our backpack. People other than our parents also put rocks in our backpacks. All of these rocks get heavier and heavier, dragging us down. As we continue, you will see that my story shows examples of several varying wounds.

For now, let's think about that heavy backpack full of rocks. What does God say about these rocks that drag us down?

"Nevertheless, I will bring health and healing to it; I will heal my people and will let them enjoy abundant peace and security." (Jeremiah 33:6)

God spoke this message to the people of Israel, who were deep in sin and experiencing God's wrath. However, in the middle of that darkness, God made a surprising promise: He would restore Israel and cleanse them of their sins, pointing to Jesus Christ as their ultimate salvation.

I believe that these promises and this verse applies to us, too! God can heal any of our wounds, self-inflicted or inflicted by others. He wants us to have abundant peace, but we have to open the door for Him.

What does that mean? That means that we have to confess that we have wounds. We must confess that we've sinned and take every sin and wound to Jesus Christ and ask Him for help. He promises us that He will answer and forgive our sins.

"If we confess our sins, He is faithful and just and will forgive us our sins and purify us from all unrighteousness." 1 John 1:9 (NIV)

What an amazing guarantee. Jesus' death provided justice for our sins, and now that He has risen to life, we can be sure of this. That triumphs over any and every wound we have!

However, the process doesn't stop there. The first step is recognizing our wounds, our problems, and our addictions, but the second step is just as important. We have to reach out for help. Reach out to someone you trust and feel comfortable confessing your wounds to. Someone like a close friend, a counselor, or a trusted family member. Transparency is vital.

Considering what I learned in the bar, I thought that vulnerability was a sign of weakness. A lot of people think that way, but we have to destroy that lie. That lie keeps us isolated and drowns us in our addictions, but admitting we have wounds and asking for help is a sign of strength.

After you ask for help, it's important to keep a few aspects in mind. Healing is a process and there's no fixed timeline. It could take a year for me to work through healing, but for someone else it could take several years. There's nothing shameful about that. However, when you see progress in your healing, you will start to experience true happiness.

More importantly, with the help of Christ, you will experience joy. Joy is a deep happiness of the soul, more permanent than a fleeting pleasure or emotion. You will see life from a different perspective. You'll see it through the healthy eyes of Christ and not through your damaged past. You will experience freedom in your mind, heart, and actions. You won't be perfect, but you will rest in the certainty that Christ has set you free!

CHAPTER 2

The thief comes only to steal and kill and destroy;
I have come that they may have life and have it to
the full.

John 10:10 (NIV)

The Inevitable Question

My sister, Estela, and I were best friends growing up. The older we got, the more I felt responsible to protect her from the trafficking and prostitution that thrives on poor families like ours. But what's an eleven-year-old boy going to do?

I decided I better make some friends bigger and meaner than me. I ended up getting to know a guy a few years older than me who lived in a nearby neighborhood. I was funny and he was twice my size. Like it has been said, opposites attract, so our relationship worked. We talked about everything.

That's what I thought, at least. One night, he brought up the one topic we'd never discussed.

He asked, "What do you know about sex, Ariel?"

Taken off guard I replied, "Nothing. I hear my dad's friends talk about it, but I don't get it."

"Don't worry, I can teach you."

I hung on his every word about sex. It wasn't long before he asked the inevitable question.

"Want to have sex with me?"

I still remember everything about that moment from the look on his face, the tone in his voice, to the feeling in my soul. I didn't want to give in. I wanted to reject him and leave, but he had a hold on me and my emotions that I still don't fully understand. Maybe it's because I looked up to him so much. Maybe it's because most of what I knew about sex came from him. Maybe it's because I wanted to be a man and, other than my dad, he was one of the only other "men" I really knew.

"Yes." I hesitated. "I'll have sex with you."

The destruction immediately began. As soon as it was over, guilt and shame overpowered me. I thought this friend would help me become a man, but instead, I felt like I had lost all the manhood that I'd wanted so badly. Confusion filled my thoughts and brokenness filled my emotions.

I didn't really understand what happened to me or what I should do, but the inner damage left me sure of one thing: I needed to grow up fast and become a man, no matter what it took. Maybe that would cover over this pain. If I stepped into manhood, that would hide this brokenness that ate away at me.

"If you show weakness, you're no man."

My dad never talked about his weaknesses. Neither did his friends. I couldn't cry or talk about anything that hurt my feelings, but at the same time, I probably couldn't start talking about what happened to me without crying. I guess that meant I couldn't talk about it at all.

Vulnerability wasn't part of manhood. Instead, I had to be strong, not just for myself, but for my sister and little brothers. Even when I told myself that, the brokenness grew each day. New terrifying thoughts entered my mind. "I don't want to live."

I had to compensate for this somehow. I had to prove to the world and to myself that I could be a real man.

"A real man knows how to get a woman into his bed. He can get any woman that he wants."

A man had sex with women.

"Talk about how they look. Their breasts, their butts. When you're not seducing them, treat them like servants. They're only good for cooking and cleaning. Women are bad people, so you only use them for your own gain."

I didn't understand all of it at the time, but I could tell that having sex with women was a large part of being a man. So, that's what I started to do.

There was a "tradition" of graduating to manhood, in which a guy's friends paid a prostitute at a local bar to have sex with him. I walked into the musty bar and found her waiting for me. She took me to the back of the bar. I barely knew how to do any of this, but I figured that I'd try. Each one of my attempts to "seduce" her made me even more uncomfortable.

Long story short, that experience didn't restore anything. I walked out feeling worse than when I walked in. I still felt the brokenness eating away and I felt a yearning for something more, but I didn't know how to fix it. The one act that I thought would make me feel like a man didn't.

The men at the bar didn't know any better. My father didn't know any better. So, neither did I.

Maybe one woman wasn't enough? Maybe I needed more. The more women I got into bed with, the more of a man I'd become. Maybe that's the lifestyle I needed to reach. No matter what I had to say, no matter what I had to do, I needed to get into bed with them.

My situation and my attitude spiraled out of control. First, I kept going to the local bar with my dad and believing what his friends told me "manhood" was. Now, don't get me wrong, these men weren't evil or intentionally trying to point me in this direction. They were just as lost as I was because that type of manhood was all they knew. However, their words taught me a wrong, painful lifestyle.

Second, I dove into unhealthy sexual relationships. I still felt like that would redeem my molestation and my poor performance with the prostitute. Sadly, I got better and better at luring these women in as I practiced. My heart hardened toward them and I didn't really see them as individuals with thoughts, feelings, and worth. Once I got them, I didn't treat them right.

I once said to a woman, "You smell terrible."

I was fifteen and the loud music didn't drown out my statement. Our dancing slowed down and the face of the girl across from me changed. I saw tears well up in her eyes.

It wasn't just the words, but how I said them. I wanted them to hurt her. Even when her friends confronted me about it a few minutes later, I was just as rude to them.

"Never keep a woman around. If you let her mooch off you long enough, she'll cheat on you. A real man doesn't get cheated on."

I needed to cheat on them first. That would get rid of these evil creatures. This sickening way of thinking didn't seem right to me, but I didn't know better. I felt like this lifestyle was killing me, but I buried any conviction, perceiving it as weakness. Women reached out for help, but real men didn't need to.

When I was seventeen, I started a relationship with a girl I truly enjoyed spending time with. I wanted to do it right, but unfortunately, a lifestyle of casual sex doesn't go away that easily. If only I had the hope I have now, but that was still years away.

We were really happy together, but one night changed that. We went to a beach party with some friends and it all started out good. She enjoyed herself and so did I, but I felt drawn to a bar a few blocks away. I left our group and it wasn't long before I was drinking inside that bar.

As soon as I started drinking, I fell back into my old

lifestyle. I started dancing with girls in the bar, eventually dancing very closely to one of them.

"Ariel! What are you doing?!"

My girlfriend found us. I know now that she had every right to be furious.

"What's the big deal? You need to chill out."

Back then, I didn't understand.

To that she responded, "We're through. I'm not putting up with this crap."

Instead of apologizing and trying to mend our relationship, I let her leave and continued my vicious cycle of partying with different girls. I would still drink, dance, and party every night. Every morning, I would be overwhelmed with guilt and shame.

I felt completely empty and lost, but I didn't know how to process that. I still didn't know who I was.

Lessons Learned

Remember how I mentioned that rocks can be placed in our backpack by people other than our parents in the last chapter? Obviously, I was no exception to that. My heaviest rock was the sexual abuse that I endured when I was eleven. Every rock that I placed in my backpack after that was a direct consequence of that traumatizing incident.

Those consequences lasted for the next twenty-five

years of my life. As you read in this chapter, I tried to compensate for the abuse instead of telling someone. If I reached out for help back then, think about how my situation would've changed. I wouldn't have wounded so many people, including the women in this chapter. I wouldn't have wounded myself. God worked in all of it for my good, but a huge portion of my story is the consequences of my decisions and sins.

Those decisions came from my stubbornness. I had to "be a man", so I refused to reach out for help. I'm sure that we all can think of someone who should've reached out for help, but didn't, so their life spiraled downhill.

I don't want you to be that person. What does God say about reaching out for help?

"Carry each other's burdens, and in this way, you will fulfill the law of Christ." Galatians 6:2 (NIV)

That implies that we have to open up about our burdens, right?

If I would've found someone to talk with about my wounds and struggles, I would've spared myself and many others so much heartache. If you have a person in your life that you know you can talk to about anything, I encourage you to go and tell them what's weighing on your heart. I know it may be terrifying, but I promise that it's worth it.

If you don't have that person, I encourage you to search for that person. There are resources in this book that can help you. Maybe there's someone that you haven't opened up to before, but you consider them trustworthy.

Don't stop with that person, either. We all need a person we can trust, a professional counselor, and spiritual help to overcome these obstacles.

What if we don't reach out and open up about our wounds?

You've already seen the beginning of the answer to that question in this chapter, so obviously, there are consequences. We start out by convincing ourselves that whatever we're doing isn't wrong. We think that we're invincible and can handle our problems on our own. Even if you don't consciously say or think this, your actions may represent that attitude.

However, those attitudes are lies and they don't last forever. Eventually, the true nature of these beliefs reveal themselves. We hurt our family and may even lose them. Many of us get to the point where we want to take our own life.

By God's grace, we can be saved from all of that. I'm using my story to warn you that when we try to handle our pain on our own, our actions can lead to irreversible consequences.

CHAPTER 3

As iron sharpens iron, so one person sharpens another.

Proverbs 27:17 (NIV)

Mentorship

E ven though I hadn't found my identity and had a lot of broken relationships because of that, not all of my relationships were unhealthy, and that is all because of God's grace. Around the age of seventeen or eighteen, I began working at a metal factory where I met Tito Ruiz. He was my new manager and just moved here from Argentina.

Meeting Tito was a miracle, even when I didn't know that at the time. I instantly connected with him and he began coaching me through life. He wasn't perfect, but he understood true manhood. Really, he became my first actual father figure.

Now, there were still a lot of tough times ahead, but I learned a lot of lessons from Tito that wouldn't make sense until later. Tito pointed out things that I'd never considered.

"If your father is addicted to alcohol, that could easily be passed on to you, Ariel. Any substance is dangerous, especially when there's a family history. You have to face that."

Not only that, but Tito also taught me new lessons about how a man should look at himself.

"A man should have confidence, but he can't be arrogant. Every man will have to humble himself at some point in his life."

The men at the bar never mentioned humility being a quality of a man, but Tito's example showed me how humility didn't mean weakness. Instead, Tito's humility caused him to look out for me! He was still confident in his values, but thought of others before himself.

"A man should stand up for himself, but that doesn't always look like flying fists. A man can stand up for himself in a way that respects the other person."

Finally, after all these years of broken relationships, there was some light in my life. I wish that I had taken better advantage of it.

Despite Tito's mentorship and love, I never shared my deep pain with him. I wanted to tell him how I'd been abused and all of my poor decisions since, but I couldn't bring myself to go through with it. As much of a good example that Tito was, my old idea of manhood was still too ingrained in my head.

Lust still dominated my life. I continued going down the path of drinking every night and having casual sex with different women. Eventually, one instance caused me to hit a new low. Everything started like all the other nights. I was dancing at a nightclub and met an attractive young lady.

Of course, my motive from the start was to have sex with her by the end of the night, but she didn't know that, and, in my mind, she didn't need to know. 4:00 a.m. arrived. "Hey, want to blow this place with me?"

She agreed.

Little did either of us know how destructive those decisions would be. We didn't go back to my place or to a hotel or anything like that. No, we ended up underneath a bridge by some train tracks in the middle of the night. We had unprotected sex right under that bridge.

After it was over, I followed my instincts. "I'm going to get out here." I thought to myself.

I left her there and never spoke to her again because I got what I wanted. I did exactly what I was taught to do with women: Sweet talk them and have sex with them. However, that certainly doesn't justify my actions. I greatly regret nights like these and take full responsibility for them. I had no idea how much they were destroying me or these young women.

My downward spiral continued and it left me feeling worse and worse. After any night of partying, I would wake up and stare at the ceiling. Shame, guilt, unhappiness, and emptiness crushed my chest as I laid in my bed. There was zero satisfaction to ease the pressure. If anything, my satisfaction decreased with each night and morning spent in my bed.

The hole in my heart grew to a point where sex with all these different women didn't satisfy me. I started searching for something else to fulfill my craving and numb the pain.

It didn't take long for me to stumble onto magazines that contained plenty of inappropriate pictures of women. A whole new world opened up with all the pleasure of sex but without any of the sweet-talking efforts. Pornography.

I didn't see anything wrong with it at first. It seemed like a normal activity for a man and it seemed like it would help me become a man. Addiction set in almost instantly and I looked at it every week. Simultaneously, my sadness and anxiety increased, especially after I just looked at porn.

Soon, I again laid on my bed, thinking about how I didn't want to live. I felt like I shouldn't live. I didn't care about anything. I didn't understand why I felt that apathy toward life because it seemed like it came out of nowhere. Now, I know it was because of pornography and its effects on my brain.

Pornography also changed how I viewed women in reality. I began to believe that one woman wouldn't satisfy me. Porn taught me that I needed to take my sex life to the next level, which looked like sleeping with two women at once. I told myself that's what I had to do to be a better man. This pathetic goal became my life mission.

My addictions and wounds were eating me alive, but as a man, I felt like I couldn't open up to anyone. Instead, I began lying as much as I needed, even to cover up other lies, to get what I wanted. I lied to get the approval of women and became a poser, putting on a fake front to impress. Looking back today, I don't know how I survived. I can only say that it was by God's grace.

Lessons Learned

First, I can't overstate the importance of a mentor. I didn't confide in Tito as much as I should've, but even without that, God used him in incredible ways to shape my life. It's so important for all of us to have someone that we can look up to.

That person won't be perfect, but they should be someone ahead of us in life who lives their life in a Godly way. A mentor should be someone who we can relate to but who's also not afraid to challenge us and speak the truth, much like how Tito spoke the truth about my family history to me.

I wish that I'd taken advantage of our relationship more. As you probably noticed, I didn't open up to him about my wounds, and I'd encourage you to make the opposite choice. If someone shows intentionality and asks you about your life, even about the hardest parts of your life, honor that and answer them honestly.

Again, we're stubborn, so it's easier said than done, but it is so powerful to allow someone wiser and more experienced to guide you through those dark times. They probably have thoughts, words of encouragement, and experiences that we would've never known about if we didn't reach out to them. Unfortunately, I didn't pursue that with Tito. Instead, I dove deeper into sexual immorality and faced one of my biggest obstacles alone: Pornography.

I described some of pornography's effects in the first part of this chapter, but all of that demonstrates how pornography rewires our brains. Sure, it starts out as a pleasurable indulgence, but it quickly turns into addiction. As that addiction eats away at our hearts and minds, we naturally lose hope in life and slip into a state of depression.

It's unavoidable that, if you don't reach out to Christ and others for help, pornography will take you down. One of the worst parts is that this is a heavy rock that I chose to put in my backpack. The heaviest rocks had been placed there by others, but this one changed everything and it was all my decision. Unfortunately, society doesn't have an issue with pornography, so it was easy for me to gain access to it.

We have to be careful with anything that's available to us. Society doesn't comprehend the impacts of pornography and its widespread use is ignored. Many children, teenagers, and adults have become addicted, especially because it's often being shoved in our faces through television and movies, the internet, social media, magazines, and more.

Some may argue that pornography only affects men, but that's no longer valid. Several years ago, the industry changed their strategy, creating "romantic" porn to attract more female viewers. If we look around and are honest with ourselves about what we see and experience, we can see that their strategy is working. All kinds of people are addicted to porn.

Most people would never admit that they've watched porn. I know I wouldn't admit it for most of my life. It's an uncomfortable sin to confess, but that is how the enemy keeps us isolated in darkness. However, what God says about this topic is pretty straightforward.

"Flee from sexual immorality. All other sins a person commits are outside the body, but whoever sins sexually, sins against their own body." (1 Corinthians 6:18)

How do we flee? Well, I think there are a few practical steps we can take to do that. First, as I said before, we confess the sin to God and ask for forgiveness. He already knows our hearts and the mistakes we've made; there's no fear in taking it to Him because Jesus took the punishment for this sin on the cross, just like He took any and every other sin. Just several verses above in 1 Corinthians 6, verse 11, points out how we were sexually immoral but we have been washed, sanctified, and justified in Christ's name and by the Holy Spirit.

Second, we confess the problem to the right person. Maybe that's a mentor or maybe it's a trusted friend. We tell them what we told God. Third, we ask for help. We ask for help from our mentors. We ask for accountability and we find resources and wisdom to help take this problem down. There's a lot of help out there, but we have to ask for it for anyone to know that we need the help and are willing to accept it.

Fourth, we identify our triggers. What causes us to turn to pornography? Sometimes, it's something that we see online and we need to do everything we can to remove access to that, such as accountability software or the app that leads us to those triggers. It could even be something we see in a physical setting that we then need to remove ourselves from. Sometimes, it goes deeper than we think. It could be a feeling of inadequacy, stress, discouragement, a hard day, or anything that the enemy uses to cause us to feel like we need some sort of relief or pleasure. Then, we remove those triggers by taking those thoughts and feelings to God and others. We learn healthy ways to process them.

Finally, as we continue to fight this sin, we have to deal with our wounds too. Using pornography is a symptom of deeper issues. We have to confess our wounds to God and to others, opening up about trauma or deep fears. Again, the freedom we find in that is invaluable, and God uses that openness to give us His strength against pornography.

Just like there are consequences when we don't address our wounds, there are consequences when we don't address pornography in our lives. The list of consequences is endless, but here are several to consider. First, we can see from Scripture that it is from the devil and a serious sin, so if we indulge it, we are not honoring God, who saved us. Second, we are reprogramming our brains. We are losing hope every time we give in and we are learning to only feed this addiction. We change our sexual behavior because of this, causing normal sex with our spouse to no longer be pleasurable. We long for an experience that isn't even real, an experience that isn't right and can never exist.

Third, as we lose hope and continue in this secret sin, we are isolating ourselves from the world and the people who care about us. We may lie to hide it and cover our tracks, which further separates us from community. Ultimately, all of this leads to depreciation. We value ourselves less and less until we feel completely worthless and even suicidal. Pornography can cause all of this because of the effect it has on our brain, like cocaine or another heavy drug. If pornography is that similar to a drug addiction, it is clear that we need to take it down and can only do that in God's power and with others at our side.

CHAPTER 4

but those who hope in the LORD will renew their strength. They will soar on wings like eagles; they will run and not grow weary, they will walk and not be faint.

Isaiah 40:31(NIV)

No Turning Back Now

Although my unhealthy addictions and life of deceit continued, God still blessed me with bright spots as I headed into my early twenties. I began a serious relationship with a young woman and I wanted this one to last. Wherever she went, I wanted to be with her.

One day she told me, "I'm moving to Georgia at the end of the year."

Turns out my dedication would be put to the test.

"I'll go with you," I said, "I just want us to be together, even if it's in the U.S."

Quickly, my motivation changed. The economy of Uruguay collapsed early in 2002, so going to America went from being a move of love to being a move of necessity. My parents had separated, so my mother and brothers needed financial help. The United States could give me what Uruguay currently couldn't: A job.

Unfortunately, in April, just a few weeks before I was supposed to leave, my plans hit a snag. My girlfriend and I broke up after she found me cheating on her. I was no longer welcome to join her in Georgia.

"A real man protects and provides for his family."

I still wanted to be a man, so I decided to still travel to America. I just changed my destination. My cousin had a friend living in New York City, so I had the idea that he could help me. One week before I would leave my home and go to this completely different place, I changed my flight from Atlanta to JFK Airport.

Getting to America wasn't an easy goal. I still had no money, and obviously, you need money to travel. The day before I was supposed to leave, everything started weighing down on me. I thought to myself, "I can't make a life there. I'm a kid off the streets of Uruguay. Who am I kidding?"

As close as I came, something kept me from cancelling my flight. My thinking changed. "I can't even make a life here, so I might as well go. My family needs this."

Ultimately, it was God at work. I called one of my best friends, he delivered vegetables for a living, and he loaned me fifty dollars. When he loaned me the money he said, "Don't waste it, Ariel. I want you to get to the U.S."

No turning back now. I still needed to get to the airport in Montevideo. My Uncle Gabriel agreed to give me a ride to the city limits, but even that had some bumps in the road. Literally.

The car was accelerating and I started yelling, "You're

going to crash; you're going to crash! Why aren't you stopping?!"

My uncle, as calm as can be, replied, "Brakes are out."

"What?!" I shouted.

We barely made it to the city. After we did make it, I thought that the next ride I'd arranged with my friend, Eugenio, would be a relief. As was the trend in my life up to this point, I thought wrong. My friend drove a large truck loaded with vegetables, which isn't an ideal taxi to the airport, but that wasn't the main problem.

Here we go again. The truck started accelerating and I shouted, "Why aren't you slowing down?! We're in the middle of the city, man!"

And again, I received a calm reply. "Sorry, Ariel, brakes are out."

I huffed, "You've got to be joking."

I worried that I'd lose my life before even making it onto the plane. Miraculously, I somehow made it to the airport and prepared to board the plane. I called my cousin, Mariano, and asked him to contact his friend on my behalf.

"Okay, when will you land in New York?" He asked.

"My first plane leaves in less than an hour."

He didn't like that answer. Mariano yelled into the phone, "What?! You're crazy! I can't get a hold of him and work all this out that fast!"

I pleaded with him, "Please, man, you've got to try. If you don't, I'll be lost in the biggest city in the U.S."

The thought of being homeless in this foreign country terrified me, but like I said before, I couldn't turn back. My sister got married, this made my mother a single mom of two little twin boys. They needed me to make it to New York City so that I could provide for them. That outweighed my fears, so I asked my cousin to still try. I left Uruguay not knowing where I was going to lay my head the next night or any night thereafter.

When I made it to a layover in Brazil, I called my cousin again. He told me he had not heard anything from his friend yet, but he was trying his best. My worst fears were being realized. Then, even though I didn't know God at that time, another miracle happened. I called Mariano right before I boarded the plane.

"Any luck? Probably not, I know, but I'm about to board my last flight."

With excitement in his voice Mariano replied, "Ariel, it's your lucky day! I just talked to him. He said you could stay with him. You'll have to find your own way there, but you have a place to go!"

Once the plane touched down in New York, I had another set of obstacles. I had to make it through customs and security without knowing any English. I still only had fifty dollars and I had to make my own way to this place where I would be staying. As another act of God's grace, I happened to be in a security line with a Cuban officer who spoke Spanish. He helped me get through the line. He then asked me how much money I had for my trip. I told him I had 450 dollars. That was a lie. I felt like something had finally gone right. I was in America! I left the airport overjoyed.

I flagged down a taxi driver and hesitantly climbed in, trying to explain where I needed to go in a way that an English-speaker would understand.

"Oh, you need to get to Grand Central Station?" He asked.

"You speak Spanish?" I said surprised.

God continued to show his favor.

He took me to Grand Central Station and charged me forty-five dollars, leaving me with only five. As happy as I was, my situation still didn't look great.

I tried to find a police officer who spoke Spanish at Grand Central Station. Thankfully, I was taken to a very kind Puerto Rican officer. He took me to the ticket window and I handed over my last five dollars.

"That's all I have. I could come back and repay you after I get settle…"

Before I could finish he stopped me and said, "Don't worry about the rest of this guy's ticket. I got it. Just get him to Beacon."

I was so grateful. I was finally on my way to my new home.

My new accommodations were with some friends of a

friend. I slept on their couch and was as grateful as I could be.

The next day, I started my new job as a dishwasher at a five-star restaurant in Cold Springs, New York. I finally would make money that I could send back home to my mother and brothers. Not only that, but my gracious host, Juan, and his sister, Angela, took me to buy the uniform I needed. They also graciously bought me underwear and socks, since I'd come to the United States with barely any clothes.

I felt like I was born again. Everything seemed like it would get better because I was in America and making money. Unfortunately, I wasn't really born again, and as my new life felt more normal, my old addictions and wounds returned.

Again, I woke up in the mornings and stared at the ceiling. Guilt and shame held me down, even though I was thousands of miles away from where I first met them. All of this was amplified because I was now in a strange land with barely any friends. Despite all this, the biggest change was yet to come. I was about to meet someone who would change my life.

Lessons Learned

After years of carrying all these rocks in my backpack, I thought I would finally get a little bit of relief by coming to America. I had the opportunity to chase the American dream, so that means I could dump all the rocks out, right? Wrong, but I didn't know that at the time. I thought that simply showing up to America would make all my problems go away. I didn't really consider tangible goals or have a vision. I just wanted to live there and make money for my family.

Don't get me wrong, that's not a bad goal, but something important for every aspect of our lives is considering what our goals are and how to get there. A ministry called Family-iD, which we will talk more about later, teaches that a way to do that is by writing our goals down. If we write them down, they become more visible and in turn, more attainable.

What does God say about goals? Does He care about goals or plans?

"Put your outdoor work in order and get your fields ready; after that, build your house." Proverbs 24:27 (NIV)

God does care about our goals and He cares about our plans to get there. This proverb shows that He wants us to make plans, and properly prepare to bring those plans to fruition, before we dive into the work itself.

First, write down your vision and your dreams. What's your ultimate destination? Second, write down your individual goals to achieve that vision. Place the goals where you can see them. Third, take action! Take the needed steps to chase your dreams and don't give up. Handle it one day at a time, striving in any way you can.

Fourth, be ready to fail. I know that sounds negative compared to the previous steps, but there's going to be obstacles to achieving anything, and sometimes, we make mistakes. Life's not about failing, though. Life's about learning from those mistakes and moving forward, better than ever.

Finally, and most importantly, remember what's truly important. If you have the choice between failing your family or failing professionally, fail professionally. Your walk with God and your relationships with those around you are far more important than any dream or goal. When it comes to relationships, sometimes, you only have one chance. Make little mistakes there, even if it means you have to make more mistakes professionally. All of that may seem overwhelming, but there's wisdom in living out those steps. If we don't, then there are a variety of consequences that we could experience.

First, we'll walk aimlessly, living life with no purpose. We won't have any direction that we want to go in, especially without any spiritual goals. We may even feel worthless and like we have nothing to accomplish if we don't keep God's love and plans for us in mind. Second, even if we do have goals, it is almost impossible to attain them if we don't take time to establish the needed steps to get there. That's why writing them down is monumental.

If we walk aimlessly and don't attain our goals, that can influence our relationships. Our purposeless way of living bleeds into how we run our family and look at our relationships. We can hurt those around us in a multitude of ways by not grounding ourselves in God and what He wants us to pursue.

CHAPTER 5

Be devoted to one another in love. Honor one another
above yourselves.

Romans 12:10 (NIV)

As He Loved Us

A few months after my drastic move to America, I met a breathtakingly beautiful woman at a restaurant. The kind of woman that was clearly out of my league.

We introduced ourselves and she told me that her name was Camila. She lived in Colorado, but she was in town visiting her brother.

We spent the whole evening talking and getting to know each other. I was instantly physically attracted to Camila and liked everything about her. I wasn't just attracted to her physically. From the moment we started talking, I could tell that she had a sincere heart.

The connection was mutual. We hit it off from the start and felt something special between us. She soon returned to Colorado and we exchanged phone numbers to keep in touch. I couldn't wait to talk to her again. Out of all the women that I met, and even dated, there had never been anyone like her. I wanted to get to know her, for her.

Unfortunately, that didn't happen as fast as I wanted. I tried to call her the following week, but no answer. I didn't hear from her for the next ten months. Things changed when, by the grace of the Lord, Camila called one of my friends, who happened to be dating Camila's brother. They told her that my birthday was coming up and that she should give me a call.

Camila did call me on my birthday, which was the best birthday present I could receive! Not only did we talk for a couple hours that night, but we talked for hours on the phone every day afterward and began a long-distance relationship. Every morning, I couldn't wait until the time came for our daily call. Just a few months later, she came to visit me, and I was elated.

She said, "Let's get dinner. You can tell me all about Uruguay."

We spent hours together sharing stories and getting to know each other better. I'd never experienced happiness like this before. Something about us clicked from the beginning and was progressing so smoothly, pushing my addictions and wounds into the background. Every day, our relationship got better and better. I still had to work while she was in town, but my excitement grew each day as I clocked out and rushed to see her. Soon, she had to go back to Colorado.

"I promise that I'll visit you soon, Camila. I can't go months without seeing you again."

I made good on that promise. Before too much time passed, I found myself in Colorado. This visit would permanently change our lives.

"Camila, you know that I'm in love with you. I've never felt anything like this before. Do you feel the same?"

She smiled and said, "I love you, Ariel. There's no question."

I told her, "I don't want to go back to New York."

"Then move here," she said, "Come and live with me and we won't have to deal with the distance anymore."

That seemed like a crazy offer. Too good to be true.

"Really? Are you sure?" I asked.

Confidently she said, "I want you here with me, Ariel."

A few more months passed and I did just that!

As exciting as that was, my old wounds slowly re-surfaced. Some of my insecurities came out and some of hers did as well. However, because we were still so happy, we were able to shove that down and enjoy our time together. But, on the inside, my past still wanted to eat away at me. Shortly after my move to Colorado, Camila expressed a desire to help me in another way.

In shock I said, "I can't let you do that just for me. That's more than I deserve."

She persisted, "Ariel, your visa is about to expire. That's a big deal, especially when I just got you here. I don't want to lose you."

"Marriage is a big deal, too," I said, "I don't want to use

you to meet an end."

I wanted to marry her because I loved her and I never wanted there to be any confusion about that. Soon after that conversation, Camila came home from work one day and wanted me to sit down.

"I have no doubt that I want to spend the rest of my life with you. I told you that there was no question that I loved you and there still isn't. I can't watch you get sent back to Uruguay. Ariel, will you marry me?"

I was blown away because no one had ever done anything like that for me or shown me that kind of unconditional, sacrificial love. Not many men can say they were proposed to and not many men would want that, but that didn't matter to me.

"Yes, Camila, I will marry you!"

We made an appointment at the courthouse and had a very special wedding day. Even though it was a very small ceremony, it was intimate for us. We both wept as we exchanged our vows and committed ourselves to this marriage for the rest of our lives.

"Till death do you part."

I felt like I had a fresh start and I believed the rest of my life was set. We purchased a condominium several months later and that became the home for our new family. We also got to travel to Uruguay for our honeymoon. We even had a wedding ceremony at a church with my family and friends.

As happy as I felt in so many of these moments, the

emptiness re-appeared in my heart. For a lot of people, reading that may seem confusing, because it seemed like my life was in such a great place. Regardless of my circumstances, the abuse from my past still hunted after me and tried to devour me. My old ideas of machismo manhood remained so I still hadn't told anyone about my wounds, not even Camila. Camila was an amazing light in my life, but I hadn't discovered the real light that I needed.

Lessons Learned

Once again, I felt like I found the way to dump the rocks out of my backpack. I thought that I finally had a stable chance to be happy with someone and that would take the weight off of me. Often, we use romantic relationships or marriage as a band aid on our wounds. We think that this other person can complete us and fill up what's lacking in our own hearts. Culture even teaches us that in some ways.

However, that's not reality or the other person's responsibility. No matter how great that person may be, they can't heal our wounds for us or make up for the inner shame that we feel over our flaws and mistakes. We are looking for a fulfillment in them that only Christ can give us.

What does God say about loving others?

"A new command I give you: Love one another. As I have loved you, so you must love one another." John 13:34 (NIV)

Jesus told His disciples this shortly after He washed

their feet at the Last Supper. He demonstrated a great deal of humility and pointed out their need for Him, before telling them to go out and love one another in the same way.

Keeping that in mind, notice what this verse says: As He has loved us. We follow His example and love in the wild, intimate, sacrificial manner that He loves us. We can't have that love on our own.

We have to truly embrace Christ's love and let Him wash us before we can properly love others, even our spouse. I truly believe that a part of embracing His love is letting Him into our wounds and heal them in ways only He can. Then, as Christ does that and as we love ourselves because of that, we can truly love others in a Christ-like way. We will experience true happiness and joy.

If we rush into a relationship without addressing our wounds, we are only setting ourselves up for failure. It may feel great at first, but as our wounds come back, that feeling fades. Again, we may only have one chance with relationships, so we want to do them right. We have to do them God's way.

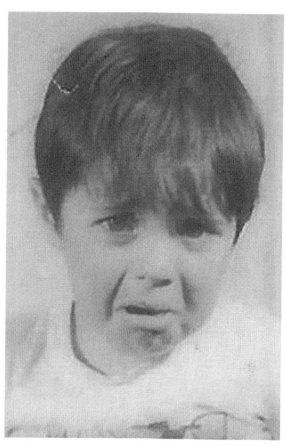

My picture from my government
ID card at age 3. (used on cover)

Me at age of 4 on the farm.

Me at age 10 at the factory.

Gregorio René Delgado Fernández
My dad taught me how to work hard,
respect others and fight for family.

The day I left Uruguay with my
mom and my sister.

Me in Colorado, I looked happy
but I was not.

Becoming a citizen of
the United States

Carmen Gladis Acevedo Noda
My mother taught me to fight for my
kids and how to overcome adversity.

The original suitcase that traveled
to the United States with me.

CHAPTER 6

Live as free people, but do not use your freedom as a cover-up for evil; live as God's slaves.

1 Peter 2:16 (NIV)

When Wounds Return

After coming back from our honeymoon, I worked diligently to suppress any feelings of emptiness or loneliness. I was still happy with Camila and she hadn't done anything wrong. I still wanted to convince myself that everything was great.

We would barbecue outside, we'd hike together, and we even enjoyed a special day exploring Pike's Peak. Our daily lives looked just as great, too, at least from the outside. I worked at a bagel place in the mornings and a Mexican cantina in the afternoons, while Camila worked at Oppenheimer Funds. Whenever I had a day off, I'd make lunch for us and ride my bike to Oppenheimer so we could eat together. When my workday would end, Camila would pick me up in her car. Our life looked perfect. But it wasn't.

Six months into our marriage, I noticed my discontentment growing and taking different forms. Camila worked with her ex-husband at Oppenheimer and I quickly became jealous. Old words started to dominate my mind.

"Never keep a woman around. If you let her mooch off you long enough, she'll cheat on you. A real man doesn't get cheated on."

Soon, they moved from my mind to my words.

I would scream, "You want to be with him, don't you?!"

In shock she gasped, "Of course not! That's ridiculous!"

She was telling the truth, but that didn't change my mind. I felt like I wasn't a good enough man for her, so she would want to be with anyone else but me. The enemy was attacking me with these old demons, but I didn't realize that then. I just focused on my inadequacy.

My jealousy was unreasonable from the second I felt it, but it only became more illogical. One day, Camila came into my work and encountered another man in the building and introduced herself to him. Instantly, I thought that she was flirting with him or trying to get with him. That was ridiculous, considering that she'd just met him, but those kinds of thoughts constantly held my mind hostage.

"You wanted him. I could see it."

Camila was in dismay. "Ariel, sweetheart, you're not thinking straight."

I continued, "Have you been seeing your ex-husband behind my back?"

She pleaded, "I love you and only you. I want to be with you and only you."

Sadly, that didn't satisfy my insecurities. The enemy's attacks continued and that sucked away all of my happiness. Every night, when I laid down in bed, the same thoughts raced through my head.

I would think, "I'm not a man. I'm not enough. Nobody will ever love me. Every person in my life will leave me. I'm broken because a man raped me. I'm broken because of my addictions. I can't tell my wife or she'll hate me."

Instead, I went back to my old coping mechanisms. I believed that Camila would cheat on me, so just like in all of my old relationships, I felt that I needed to cheat on her first. That would make us even somehow.

We hadn't even been married for a whole year before I started cheating. This sounds sickening and devastating, and it was, but I didn't even really think about it. It felt natural to stay late at work and go out on Saturday nights. It felt natural to sweet talk women, get their numbers, and sleep with them.

Every time that I started talking with a woman who wasn't my wife, I hated it. I had no desire to get into bed with this stranger.

"A real man knows how to get a woman into his bed."

This was what I needed. I needed to be a man and sleep with as many women as I could. I needed to be good enough. As the next couple of years passed, my activities didn't go unnoticed.

She would ask, "Why were you out so late last night?"

"Work was slammed." I lied.

She persisted. "Who's that woman that just texted you?"

"Someone from work. You have nothing to worry about, baby." Another lie.

I still went to bed and woke up with guilt and shame that made me feel worthless. I know that I deserved some of those consequences, but that didn't stop me from doing what seemed natural.

While the cheating continued, I also returned to my other form of lust: Porn. I would look at magazines when home alone or even when Camila was sleeping. Porn destroyed my mind when I was younger and now that destruction continued. First, it created doubts and unrealistic expectations of my sex life. The scenarios in porn were fake and I wanted to experience them in reality. I started to believe that Camila wasn't enough and couldn't meet my sexual needs.

As time went on, my porn addiction grew to the point where I looked at it daily. I continued having sex with multiple women other than my wife. All of this fed my porn and sex addiction, while eating away at my hope.

Soon, old feelings of not wanting to live resurfaced. They became worse. I thought, "I should just kill myself."

I didn't know why I hated my life so much, but now I know that my addiction to pornography played a large role in those thoughts.

Although my personal life spiraled out of control, my

professional life was improving daily. I had quit the bagel cafe and kept working at the cantina, but I started a fulltime job preparing food at Chipotle. I thoroughly enjoyed working at Chipotle and quickly realized this was where I needed to be. Apparently, the management at Chipotle agreed. I was promoted to a supervisor position within my first few months there. Training for the supervisor position also gave me the chance to take English classes, which was a huge blessing! These classes inspired me and helped me succeed in the professional world.

Shortly after that, I was promoted to assistant manager. They loved having me be a part of their team and watching me grow. As good as it felt to get these promotions, I still felt hopeless on the inside. Guilt and shame overwhelmed me daily, but I became a master at concealing those feelings and sins. For the sake of my career and my marriage, I kept a mask over these dark parts of my life, but that didn't help my soul.

Less than a year after my promotion, another amazing opportunity appeared. The general manager was transferring to another location, so they wanted me to take his place. Considering I came to America with no English and no money, this was a huge accomplishment. I spent the next six months in training before I dove into my new position. As I developed systems and employees, I felt my leadership skills grow and I watched the number of restaurants shoot from 400 to 800.

Upper management told me, "We think it would benefit you to take some college classes in Denver. You'd polish your English and learn management techniques.

We can cover the cost."

Obviously, I eagerly accepted. I mention all of these events because they did encourage me as I invested in myself, but I still couldn't reconcile my two lives. My professional life felt incredible, but my personal life was still full of deception, addiction, and the never-ending shame.

Six months after I became the general manager, my area manager came to me yet again.

He said, "Ariel, after your impressive performance, I want you to become my first restaurateur. This development position will require months of extensive training and multiple interviews, but I think you would be amazing in this role."

"I would be honored, sir."

Ultimately, all of this would culminate with an interview with Steve Ells, the founder of Chipotle, and Monty Moran, the company's CEO, as well as two other company officers. One day, they came to my restaurant and asked my employees about my leadership skills and habits. I waited in another room, fidgeting and shifting constantly. Any minute, the time for the interview would arrive.

Then, they went to a back room and called me in. As I walked in, I was in awe that these high-level businessmen wanted to come to my restaurant and speak with me, and even while I was awe-struck, I started answering their questions. Before they left, Steve Ells pulled me aside.

"The way you handle yourself is very impressive and your turn-around of this store speaks for itself. I think you're ready to become a restaurateur."

I couldn't believe it! After a couple of follow-up conversations, I received a call from both Steve Ells and Monty Moran.

"Congratulations, Mr. Delgado! You're officially a restaurateur."

My career was taking off in ways that I never would have dreamed when I was a kid. Both Camila and I were doing so well in our companies that we were able to not only buy our condominium, but also finance a car for me to use.

For a lot of people in their twenties or thirties, that wouldn't seem like a big deal. However, having grown up in Uruguay and coming to America with nothing, I traveled by walking, riding horses, riding bikes, or relying on others for rides. Buying a car was a huge step forward for me and reflected the success of my professional life. As I look back now, I see what an amazing gift from God that all of that was!

One evening, a big change took place. I came home to find Camila waiting for me.

"We need to talk."

She seemed nervous, which made me nervous. Had she discovered my porn addiction or one of the women I slept with? How would I explain myself? How could I cover myself this time? I never would have guessed what she wanted to tell me.

"Ariel, I'm pregnant."

Camila felt nervous because she didn't know how I would take the news. As shocked as I was, I felt overjoyed! We went out to celebrate that night and wanted to keep the news to ourselves, but the excitement proved to be too much for us. We called our family and friends that night and shared this miracle with them!

This news gave me a boost that helped me feel better about my life. Temporarily, my insecurities faded. I developed general managers to send out to different restaurant locations every day, and then I would come home to Camila, who would practice English with me. She proofread emails for me, which really helped me sound professional and fluent in both my speech and writing. She supported me in so many ways while pregnant, but things still weren't perfect.

Camila would plead with me, "I need you here, Ariel. I can't do this alone."

I kept going out on Saturdays with friends. I wanted to have fun, and as that desire grew, my jealousy quickly returned. I still felt guilt over cheating on Camila so much, so I deflected that guilt onto her.

"I know you're sleeping around on me!" I yelled.

She responded, "That's not true! Why won't you trust me?"

I twisted my own sin and pinned it on Camila.

One specific, devastating argument occurred during her pregnancy.

"I know you've been having an affair. Is this baby even mine?!"

I asked it out of jealousy and insecurity, but as soon as the words left my mouth, I felt ashamed. Camila could barely muster a word. Tears lined her eyes. Eventually, a gentle, shaken whisper came out of her lips. "How could you ask me that? You know that you're the father."

I instantly knew that question had the potential to ruin our marriage. She internalized that wound and carried it with her for years to come, even to this day.

Nine months came to a close and Camila gave birth to our beautiful daughter, Angelina. I had the privilege of being in the room with Camila. The nurse looked at me beaming and said, "Would you like to be the first one to hold her?"

The nurse handed me a beautiful, precious sight. Seeing her and holding her started a fire in my heart, restoring a light to my life. I would change. I would leave these flaws and addictions behind for the sake of my wife and daughter. I would be the man that they needed. After taking Angelina and Camila home, I succeeded at getting rid of my dangerous habits. Too bad it didn't last.

Before long, the demons returned and preyed on me. I quickly gave in, looking at porn again. This was the start of a domino effect, as porn led to sleeping with other women, just like before. Once again, I made my situation worse. I began a long-term affair with a co-worker at Chipotle.

Camila caught on to this quickly. She would often bring Angelina to Chipotle to eat with me in the months after giving birth, and every time she came in, my co-worker treated Camila poorly by being extremely rude to her. Camila also found several phone calls from her on my phone, leading to a confrontation.

"You're talking to her a lot. Are you having an affair?"

Again, I lied, "Absolutely not! I work with her, so obviously we're going to talk."

She persisted, "Are you sure?"

"You're crazy for thinking that I would ever cheat on you, Camila. That's insane."

Her voice grew quiet. "Okay."

She knew that I was lying. No matter how much I tried on my own to change or cover myself, my marriage was slowly coming undone.

Now, like I said before, I became good at hiding my addictions and cheating lifestyle. I lied constantly, covering lies with other lies, but no one can live like that forever. Eventually, I became sloppy, leaving text messages on my phone. Camila never questioned me again, but I always believed that she knew what I was doing. The tension between us only intensified as the years passed.

All of this caused guilt and shame to tighten their chains around me, but I still couldn't bring myself to tell Camila or anyone else. A real man wouldn't confess. Everything, from the actions to their consequences, weighed me down and kept me in slavery.

Lessons Learned

As you can see, professional development and a growing family didn't fix my wounds. These were great blessings, but again, I thought that they were the cure. When I held my daughter for the first time, I thought that I'd never be unhappy again. As I climbed up in Chipotle, I felt like I should be happier.

That mindset is an example of how lost I was. I assumed that unhappiness was the real problem in my life. If I could be happy, I'd stop feeling insecure, I'd stop cheating, and I'd be an amazing husband and father. However, unhappiness was not the problem. It was just a symptom of my deeper wounds.

I thought that happiness could be found in the world. My circumstances looked great, so why didn't I wake up happy? All of us fall into that mindset at times. We want to change our circumstances so that we can be content. We think that if this one situation goes in a positive direction, our lives will suddenly be perfect.

That is an unrealistic and illogical belief. Happiness and being content doesn't have that much to do with the world. Being content, and having true happiness and joy, starts in our hearts. However, we can't really have that unless we remove all of the pain in our hearts, and we remove that pain by running to Christ and others.

What does God say about this topic?

"I know what it is to be in need, and I know what it is to have plenty. I have learned the secret of being content in any and every situation, whether well fed or hungry, whether living in plenty or in want. I can do all this through him who gives me strength." Philippians 4:12-13 (NIV)

The last verse is famously quoted, but it's easy to miss the meaning. Paul wrote this from prison and said he is content no matter what! Doesn't that go against what the world tells us? The world tells us to not be content or happy until we get what we want. God tells us the opposite.

I encourage you to remember that happiness can never be found in the world. Instead, we need to ask why we're trying to find it in our circumstances. Many times, the answer takes us back to those wounds. If the answer takes us back to our wounds, we need to go to our trusted people and share those struggles.

Once again, having someone in our corner is monumental, especially because seeking happiness in the world is such an easy mistake to make. Without addressing these tendencies and wounds, we risk all our relationships. Trying to find happiness in our circumstances or even in our family members adds a burden that's difficult for all to escape.

CHAPTER 7

But now that you have been set free from sin and have become slaves of God, the benefit you reap leads to holiness, and the result is eternal life.

Romans 6:22 (NIV)

Enough of Being a "Man"

My selfish, stupid decisions continued, even though my marriage was falling apart. I continued my affair with my co-worker and often ended up in situations where the three of us had to be in the same room, such as a going-away party for one employee, a baby shower for another, and the annual Christmas party. Camila didn't have to come.

"She's going to be there, isn't she?" Camila would ask. "I told you before, you have nothing to worry about! I want you there, baby. I want my wife at my side."

With doubt in her eyes she would whisper, "Okay."

I wanted her there out of selfishness and pride. Nothing more.

The tension thickened every time that we were all together. Camila and my co-worker would exchange glances and the occasional glare. However, because I was still so caught up in myself and my own problems, I didn't do a thing to stop it. I didn't think about anybody but myself.

Even while married and having an affair, I still felt so inadequate and I craved something more. The hole in my heart kept growing and I barely felt like a man. I continued to try to compensate by going to nightclubs and talking to other women.

Why hadn't I figured out that this didn't make me feel better or make me any more of a man? I didn't know anything else. These were the solutions that I was taught in that old bar and that I had tried out again and again. However, at the end of 2010, yet another opportunity for change presented itself. Upper management reached out to me again.

"Ariel, we would like you to oversee all of our Oklahoma locations, as well as some of our Kansas locations. It would require you and your family to move to Oklahoma City."

Just like every other time that I had moved or had a change in circumstance, I saw this as a chance for a clean slate. I could leave my past and my addictions behind, while moving forward with my family. As much as I deserved the guilt, I was sick of it. I desperately wanted to become a better man, husband, and father.

We moved to Oklahoma and purchased a new home. Things started out great, just prior to our move, we had our second daughter, Juliana. I left the cheating and insecurities in Colorado, but once again, they shortly followed me to Oklahoma.

I know now that it was the enemy attacking me, regardless of life circumstances, but I didn't understand that back then. I kept remembering my past. I'd made so many mistakes and drowned in a vicious cycle of casual sex. I woke up every morning and stared at the ceiling, thinking the same old things. I would think, "My manhood was taken from me. I can never recover from this. I am worthless."

I turned back to porn and partying to cope. I once again cheated with multiple women, resuming my double life. I lived this disgusting lifestyle for a total of twelve years, eight in Colorado, and four in Oklahoma. Then, like with any lie and sin, one day it crashed and burned. Lies and sin are always exposed and mine were no exception.

It was February 5th, 2016.

Camila came to me and said, "Ariel, we need to talk."

I knew that it wasn't good. "What's wrong, honey?"

"I think we both know. I'm tired of living like this," she said, expressing more honesty in her voice and in her eyes than I'd noticed in a long time. She didn't enjoy this, but she also didn't hold back. "I want to separate. I need you to leave."

As much as her words devastated me, I couldn't argue with any of it.

"Alright. I'll leave."

I spent years hurting her, and now, the least I could do was do what she asked. Not to mention, I was exhausted from living my double life. Something had to change, so there was no point in trying to keep life the same. That didn't change how much this day hurt, though.

"Daddy, where are you going?" Angelina, now six, asked. Her innocent face displayed confusion while I packed my suitcases. Julianna, now four, didn't look any less perplexed.

Angelina cried, "Daddy, don't go!"

Noticing the pain on my daughters' faces caused everything to click in a new way. I'd felt guilt and shame for years, but not like this. Finally, I came to the complete realization of what I'd done. I destroyed my marriage by my cheating, lying, and addictions. I hurt my wife day after day through those actions. I destroyed my family by my sins. I wrecked the happy family that my girls could've had.

Around 2:00 p.m. that same day, I checked into Fairfield Inn & Suites in Oklahoma City. As I sat in my new home, the old thoughts returned and swirled around me.

"I completely failed as a man."

Not only was I worthless, but I'd driven everyone away from me. Just like I always feared. Beyond that, I still had these uncontrollable cravings. I yearned for porn, masturbation, sex, and women like someone would yearn for cocaine.

Everything seemed hopeless. I sobbed and made my decision. I needed to die. The time had come for me to literally pull the trigger. I stood from the bed and went over to my suitcases, digging around until I found the gun. I threw the clothes to the side and lifted the weapon, putting it to my forehead. Then, as my finger hovered over the trigger, I saw them.

In fact, I could only see them. My girls' faces blocked out everything around me. I still didn't believe in God back then, but somehow, He still showed His miracles. The gun fumbled out of my hands. I heard the thud as it hit the floor, but I still only saw my family.

I went back and forth for hours, but I couldn't go through with it because of their faces. I couldn't get them out of my mind. Today, I'm so grateful for that. I felt like angels surrounded me in that moment. God had a purpose for my life.

I started to reach out to a few people, such as friends or counselors. No one answered the phone. Still, old mindsets tried to regain control of my brain.

"A real man is always strong. He never shows weakness. If you show weakness, you're no man."

Those words pounded my head like fists, but I knew that if I let them have the same power, I would end my life. If I wanted to live and be there for my family, I would have to make one of the toughest decisions.

Enough of being a "man".

With nothing left to lose, except my life, I walked across the street to St. Anthony's Hospital at 2:00 a.m.

"Uh, I need help. I tried," I hesitated, "I almost tried to kill myself today. I want to kill myself."

The staff put me in a secluded room and two different doctors came to evaluate me. For the first time in my life, I openly talked about my wounds. I told them how a friend molested me when I was only eleven. How I had been addicted to sex since I was a teenager. I told them about Camila asking me to leave the house.

They responded by asking the same question a couple different times.

"Mr. Delgado, do you really want help?"

Every time, I gave the same answer.

"Yes. I came to you because I need help."

I didn't feel completely comfortable saying that, but I knew that I had no choice.

One of the doctors said, "Well, Mr. Delgado, our only real option here is to send you to Cedar Ridge Behavioral Hospital. It's a facility specializes in mental health treatment and they can give you the help you need."

They called a police officer to transport me there, and before I knew it, I was in the back of a police car. The officer was kind, and I wasn't even handcuffed, but I still felt pathetic. The drive only took thirty-five minutes, but I had never experienced a drive that felt as long as that one. I stared out the car window and wept, as the enemy put the same old lies into my mind.

"I was worthless, and I deserved to die."

In the middle of it all, I could only ask one question.

"If God existed, why did this happen? Why did all of this happen to me?"

Once we finally arrived at Cedar Ridge, I went through a lengthy check-in process. I filled out piles of paperwork, had conversations with the nurses, and was given a full physical.

The nurse asked me, "Mr. Delgado, you have no visible injuries, and your medical history doesn't indicate any mental health issues. Why did you come to Cedar Ridge?"

"I need help," I replied, "I really need help."

They admitted me, but things didn't get better instantly. The men's pavilion didn't have any space left, so I was put in a pavilion with older females. The staff made me get rid of most of my clothes, so I was only left with my t-shirt and underwear when I entered my room.

My room was purely white. The blank room held nothing except a bed. Even the sheets on the bed were different than any sheets I'd seen, so that no patient could use them to try to commit suicide. Someone checked on me every two hours, but other than that, I was completely alone. Throughout the night, I drifted back to my normal way of thinking. The thinking that became normal to me.

"I needed to die."

Little did I know that the best was yet to come. The next day, February 6th, changed my life forever.

Lessons Learned

In every chapter, I've talked about consequences, but you can really see the consequences of my actions in this chapter. The rocks in my backpack shoved me to my knees. Thanks to my addictions, I was losing everyone I loved.

Those addictions, symptoms of my deeper wounds, kept adding rocks to my backpack. Over the years, the guilt and shame grew unbearable, and when I was in that hotel room, it reached a peak.

That's always the end destination of these addictions, no matter how relieving they seem in the moment. They cause us to hate ourselves and doubt our worth. They consume us, brainwashing us into thinking that we can never stop. We feel hopeless, and sometimes, that leads to suicidal thoughts and even attempts.

Naturally, all of us want to avoid this, but these addictions can deceive us. That's why we have to recognize that we have a problem, no matter where we are at in this process. Even if we feel like we're too far gone, we need to reach out for professional help if we want anything to get better. Not only that, but we need to seek spiritual help, even if we've never had a spiritual conversation before. We need people to point us to Jesus and His redemption because that's the one thing that can overpower the guilt and shame in our hearts.

What does God say about this? Well, He has a couple of things to say.

"My sacrifice, O God, is a broken spirit; a broken and contrite heart you, God, will not despise." Psalm 51:17 (NIV)

David wrote these words after he committed adultery and murder. He experienced the consequences of his sin and his heart was shattered, but he points out something amazing: God does not despise a broken, remorseful heart that comes before Him.

"Therefore, there is now no condemnation for those who are in Christ Jesus, because through Christ Jesus the law of the Spirit who gives life has set you free from the law of sin and death." Romans 8:1-2 (NIV)

When Christ forgives our sins by His death paying the penalty and His resurrection defeating death, we are free from any condemnation. We are free from those addictions. Each one of us can rest in this truth by knowing Christ.

Even as we seek spiritual help, we have to remember to cling to these truths and stick to our plan of healing. It took time for us to allow these addictions and impulses to overpower us, so it will take time to walk away from them. However, that doesn't mean we should quit. It shows that we should persevere! If we don't seek help and Christ, we'll continue living an unhappy life. An unhappy life that takes us down a dangerous path.

CHAPTER 8

This poor man called, and the LORD heard him;
he saved him out of all his troubles.

Psalms 34:6 (NIV)

The Beginning of a New Life

I didn't know what to expect on February 6th, 2016. Cedar Ridge already had a day structured for me, but all of this came as completely new territory. My activities ranged from meals and classes, to meetings with counselors and psychiatrists. This came as a far cry from my life at bars, farms, and factories in Uruguay. Thankfully, during all of this, the facility let me make a phone call.

"Camila, I almost tried to kill myself yesterday. I'm in a mental health facility."

"Oh, Ariel."

She kindly came to visit me, but the visit didn't go as well as I would've liked.

She told me, "I want you to do what you need to get better. For our daughters."

She meant that, but I still saw the same brutal honesty in her eyes and heard it in her voice. She didn't want to try to reconcile. I didn't blame her. She had every right to feel that way. Still, it felt like a punch below the belt. I lost my wife and couldn't get her back. Again, that stole my will to live. I didn't see any light in this situation, and I doubted why I came to this bizarre place. Camila didn't want me anymore. Everyone would probably be better off if I was dead.

Before this, I never thought about God much, but if I did, I believed that he didn't care about me and wouldn't want to help me with my problems. After my poor visit with Camila, I started thinking about Him more.

When I went to bed at 10:00 p.m., I was fed up. All my emotions started pouring out. I fell onto my knees and started screaming at God. I called Him insulting names. I challenged Him and just yelled.

"If you're real, show me!"

I kept asking that same question over and over.

"Why? Why is this happening to me?!"

I wouldn't have called this praying. I didn't know how to pray. I didn't have any reverence. I kept taking my anger out on Him for the next thirty minutes. Then, something in my heart changed. Maybe He got tired of me yelling at Him. Suddenly, I felt relief. The burdens fell off my back. The same burdens and flaws that I carried on my back since I was eleven. I even heard voices.

First, I tried to deny it. I was locked in a mental hospital, so of course I was hearing voices. I was probably going crazy. My denial didn't stop the voices and the peace remained. These weren't just voices in my head. God spoke to me. Chills coursed through every part of my body and I just stared at the wall. I even started to smile.

"God, is that You?"

He confirmed it over and over, pushing past my doubts. All my life, I never felt like I could get away from my filth. Now, it literally felt like He reached inside my heart and yanked all of that out. I felt lighter than ever before when I laid down that night. When I woke up the next morning, I felt happy. I finally had a hope in something beyond my skewed vision of manhood. I had real hope.

I never liked to write, but that morning, I started writing down my new goals. I wanted to get involved in church. I wanted to get baptized. Now that I started a relationship with God, I thought that everything would instantly get better. I'm still not sure if the doctors and nurses believed me when I recounted all of this, but that didn't matter to me. I knew the living, only true God.

Five days later, I was released, and I was a totally different man than the one who walked into Cedar Ridge in the middle of the night a few days ago. Camila and her mother picked me up, and as I walked out the door, I knew that I was walking out with God at my side. I was walking out with real hope because God is hope.

Once Camila brought me back to our house, I was overjoyed to see Angelina and Julianna, hugging and kissing them both. I felt such a mixture of peace, joy, and excitement. Quickly, I was reminded of reality.

Camila later told me, "I'm glad you're okay, but my feelings haven't changed. I don't think it's good for you to be living in the house."

"I understand. If you let me stay for thirty days, I'll work on finding a permanent place to go."

"Alright," she agreed, "thirty days."

The heartache of my broken marriage re-appeared, but I still felt determined to do all that I'd written down in Cedar Ridge. I wanted to read the Bible and journal, while finding a local church. Camila actually helped me with that.

She told me, "There's that one church nearby. Life Church, I think? I heard that Kevin Durant goes there."

I decided that I'd give it a shot. As soon as I visited Life Church for the first time, I felt completely comfortable. The people there treated me like family. They barely knew me, but it seemed like they really cared about me. Everything went so well that I even asked to meet with the campus pastor, Chris Beall.

Chris agreed to meet with me in his office and it quickly turned emotional. As I cried, I explained everything that happened. Pastor Chris patiently and graciously listened to me.

"God loves you, Ariel. Jesus is walking with you through this. Something that may help you is finding one or two mentors to also walk through this with you. I know a couple men who I'd like you to meet."

Next week, I met up with Trey Dixon at a cafe in Oklahoma City. Pastor Chris referred me to Trey because Trey serves as the director of True North Ministries, an organization dedicated to encouraging and challenging men in their spiritual journey. I became emotional when I met with Trey, still feeling like a mess. None of that fazed Trey. He started coaching me right there, giving me wisdom and advice. I felt like he'd taken me under his wing without hesitation. No one had done that for me since Tito, and this was on a much deeper level.

As if that wasn't enough, Trey suggested that I try a group called Fight Club (Fighting for Marriage and Family). Men and women attend Fight Club once a week to learn about God, how to become the person your spouse needs, and how to not give up on your family. Everything sounded so new and foreign to me, but I knew that good could come from it.

I decided to attend the next Fight Club meeting, showing up early and meeting the group's leader, Greg Gunn. Greg invited me into his office, along with a couple of the group's leaders, and we talked about my story.

One of the Fight Club veterans said, "You aren't alone, Ariel. I've experienced many of those same self-doubts and harmful thoughts. We've all faced every temptation that you have, and we've all fallen a number of times."

It felt surreal. My father and his friends never wanted to show weakness because that wasn't a part of real manhood. Now, I sat in an office around a group of men who enjoyed sharing their weaknesses! The experience was very freeing. However, I still questioned some things.

"There is a purpose for your pain, Ariel," Greg said, smiling, "God has a better purpose for this than we can imagine right now!"

In fact, it almost seemed like he was excited about them. I found that a little rude. My family fell apart and I was supposed to believe that there was some mysterious purpose in all the brokenness? I even questioned Greg's constant optimism. How could someone be that positive in a terrible situation like this? Despite that, there was still something about that optimism that kept bringing me back to Fight Club. I started attending weekly.

One evening Greg said, "It is monumental to fight for your family. The world will tell you to give up on your marriage, but that's all part of a lie. As a man, you're called to lead and fight for your wife and kids, no matter what obstacle you're up against."

These teachings summarized the conflict in my head. The worldly part of me, the part that had run rampant most of my life, told me that I should give up on Camila and move on. I could find a new, better wife, and rebuild my family. Now, something else pushed back against that mentality and it made sense. Camila waited on me for twelve years, so it wasn't right for me to give up after just a few months.

Trey Dixon said, "You're on a good path, Ariel, and now's the time to dive in. Study the Word of God and meditate on it throughout the day. Attend church weekly and find ways to get involved."

Trey and Greg didn't stop fighting for me, either.

I followed their advice, and as I went to Life Church on the weekends, peace continued to come over me. The environment at the church felt so refreshing. People accept you in your brokenness and in your sin. Camila and the girls even started coming and sitting with me. I started volunteering and enjoyed every second of it. As my church involvement increased, it seemed like things were really looking up. Again, that's what it seemed like.

I didn't understand why everything around me hadn't gone back to normal. If I was on a "good path", why didn't my problems go away? Isn't that what is supposed to happen when you became a Christian?

Around that time, I also moved into an apartment in a suburb of OKC. Once again, when I went to bed and woke up alone, I repeated old thoughts and patterns.

"I needed to die."

I felt like I needed to watch porn, drink alcohol, and do whatever else I needed to make these feelings go away. I gave into these thoughts often, too. I stumbled, and I didn't get it. The conflict continued as I kept attending church and reading the Word. God still grew me, despite my struggles, and at the end of 2016, I decided that it was time to get baptized. Even though Camila and I weren't on the best of terms, she came to my baptism to support me.

Pastor Chris asked, "Ariel, have you made Jesus Christ your Lord and Savior, believing that He died for your sins and rose to life?"

"Yes, I have!"

The volunteers held my arms as I leaned back, immersing myself further in the water.

"Then I baptize you, my brother, buried with Christ in baptism…"

I was submerged for a few seconds before they excitedly lifted me back up.

"…and risen to walk in newness of life!"

The applause bounced off the walls. I felt like I was on top of the world. Maybe this was what it took to change my circumstances. Unfortunately, that's where I thought wrong.

Lessons Learned

I never wanted to end up in a hospital or mental facility. I only turned there when I felt like my life was on the line and when I had no other choice. I lost my wife, my daughters, and my home before I chose to get help.

Sometimes, we don't surrender or reach out until we hit rock bottom. Right now, I want you to know that you shouldn't wait until you hit that point. Reach out now so that you don't have to later. Spare yourself and your family the pain by crying out to God right where you are.

What does God say about reaching out for help?

"Yet the LORD longs to be gracious to you; therefore, he will rise up to show you compassion. For the LORD is a God of justice. Blessed are all who wait for him! People in Zion, who live in Jerusalem, you will weep no more. How gracious he will be when you cry for help! As soon as he hears, he will answer you." Isaiah 30:18-19 (NIV)

What God spoke to Israel in the midst of their sin is true for us today. God is longing for you; He is ready for you to cry out to Him. He won't delay in answering you. It seems like a hard step to take, especially when we realize that our wrong actions and sins have gone against God and those around us. When we humble ourselves, we find rest, just like I did that night at Cedar Ridge.

Get real and authentic with yourself and with God. Tell Him what's really on your heart and bring those wounds to the surface. Don't suffer in that darkness anymore. Instead, let God's compassion wash over you. Let the trusted person or people in your life know exactly what is going on and allow them to walk through this process with you.

I can't overstate the importance of this. If we wait until our wounds and addictions dominate us, we aren't only hurting ourselves. We're hurting the people who care about us, especially our spouses, children, and close friends. If crying out to God for help and facing our struggles helps them, we shouldn't let anything hold us back.

You may not know what to say to God. That's okay because He knows what you need. Just cry out to Jesus, even if you don't have the words. Trust in Him and discover what following Him looks like. Dive into a local church and the community there. Start reading the Bible and seeing how much He loves you and what He wants to do in your life. As Ephesians 3:20 points out, God can do immeasurably more than all we can ask or imagine according to His power at work within us. Reaching out for help shouldn't be an endpoint in your life. Reaching out for help should be only the beginning of your new life.

CHAPTER 9

But you, Lord, are a compassionate and gracious God,
slow to anger, abounding in love and faithfulness.

Psalms 86:15 (NIV)

The Wrong Expectations
of Christianity

When you become a Christian, everything is supposed to fix itself, right? Surely at some point, whether it's when you're saved or baptized, things magically change, right? Yeah, that's what I thought, too. It didn't happen that way.

I returned to work at Chipotle shortly thereafter and was still managing multiple locations and overseeing many employees. I looked successful, but life doesn't care about what you look like. Slowly, my personal trauma began to strip away my successful, high-achieving image.

My spiritual life was crackling with new life, but regardless, I felt wrong leading hundreds of people at work while I failed to first lead my family of four. Just as guilt and shame ravaged every other area of my life, they now mounted again, and not just when I laid in bed, either.

I remember driving to my restaurants and then breaking down in tears before I even went inside. I would sit in my car and drown in the shame. Sometimes, if I managed to make it inside the restaurant, I would fall apart again in front of managers.

They would ask, "Sir, are you okay?"

Sometimes, I couldn't even answer. I'd spent years climbing the ladder of success, achieving prestige in Chipotle and winning glory for myself, and now I was a sopping mess. Then, the final blow came.

Divorce papers from Camila arrived. They hung in my hands and I could barely muster the strength to flip through them. My mom, who was visiting from Uruguay, stood in my living room and nervously watched. The content was generic but seeing the end of our marriage in writing was like another punch in the stomach. My mom and I wept over the true end of my marriage.

These were the consequences of my poor choices, but I still kept asking him that same question over and over.

"I just got baptized, so why is this happening to me?"

The depression became so severe that my work situation got worse. I woke up and stared at the ceiling once again. My bed felt just as cold and uncomfortable as it did when I wrapped myself in a brick-heated sweater. My marriage was over. I lost my family. I felt like I was worthless again. I would think, "Why bother getting out of bed?"

These words repeated themselves all day every day over the next two weeks. I never got out of bed. Instead, I believed the lies of the enemy.

As time went on, I knew that my restaurants deserved

better. Better than a man who cried in bed all day. I knew that I had to face my boss. I shook as I held the phone to my ear. She seemed confused.

"Ariel, what's wrong?"

"I haven't been working. I don't know what's happening at any of the locations and I haven't known for months. I haven't even gone in for the last two weeks."

Angrily she replied, "This is bad. Very bad. You know that, right?"

"Yes. I'm sorry."

They terminated me. After years of promotions and success, I lost it all and ended up right back where I started. I felt like I hit rock bottom. I hadn't. Not yet.

Around this same time, I set up an appointment with a new counselor, Dr. Talley. During my first appointment, he gave me multiple tests to determine my level of depression.

"You scored very high on all of them, Ariel. I think it would be helpful if we worked together."

I told him, "I want to, but I don't even have a job. I have a family to take care of. I don't know if I can."

With understanding he said, "Don't worry, we can figure out finances later. I want to help you."

I continued some healthy habits. I met with Trey and Greg, volunteered at Life Church, and attended Fight Club weekly. I heard so many similar testimonies from people around me. Other members had also struggled with an addiction to pornography. I found others who had been unfaithful to their wife. Others who were sexually abused as a child. Surprisingly, I met several people who also felt like they would never be good enough.

I finally began to realize that I wasn't the only one who dealt with these issues. It started to click that I needed to share my story with others. Once again, I felt an intense conflict inside of me. I would pray to God.

"God, I want You to heal my wounds and help me leave my addictions behind."

However, the impulses of my flesh still felt natural. I even tried to go out and meet women so that we could have sex. I met a few, but before we actually got anywhere, something stopped us every time. I would end up alone on my bed once again, dwelling on my fleshly desires. Why did the door keep shutting? Greg's words came back to me.

"God has a better purpose for this than we can imagine right now!"

Maybe that wasn't as rude as I thought. Maybe I couldn't have sex with these women because God had something better. That didn't instantly make things perfect, no matter how much I wanted that to be the case.

I got a job working as a general manager at another restaurant, taking a massive pay cut. I still paid for our mortgage, rent for my own apartment, and I wanted to make sure that Camila and the girls had everything they needed each day. As the months passed, all of these bills threatened to collapse on me.

I had to tell Camila, "I think we need to sell the house. I can't afford the mortgage anymore. I'm so sorry."

Camila and the girls moved onto a rental property, while I couldn't even afford to pay my own rent or buy food for myself. All I could hope to do was pay the bills for my girls. I'd end up under a bridge if that meant Camila still had money for rent and food for our daughters, and as it turned out, I was heading for just that.

In order to still pay their bills, I packed what little belongings I had into my 1999 Chevy Silverado and moved out of my apartment. While I tried to come up with some sort of plan, I slept in my truck in the Walmart parking lot at night. I would visit my daughters every other day.

They would ask, "Daddy, why can't we come over?"

I didn't want to worry them, so I said, "I'm trying to figure some things out, sweetheart."

"But we want to stay with you!" They would exclaim.

I had to tell them the truth. "I'm not staying at my apartment anymore, honey. I'm sleeping in my truck right now, but don't worry about anything. You will always have a roof over your heads and food on the table."

I didn't want to lie, either. I needed to leave that behind.

A solution didn't seem to be close, either, at least not as 2017 came to an end. When New Year's Eve came, I again spent the night in the Walmart parking lot. I couldn't fall asleep, as my mind obsessed over my finances. I couldn't do anything to change my circumstances. I had nothing. I looked around the truck. I had no one. The only One left with me was God.

I asked, "How did I end up here, God?"

No immediate response. Frustrated I asked a familiar question again, "I don't understand! Why is this happening to me?! I'm so tired of asking You that, but nothing ever gets better!"

Finally, He gave me an answer. He revealed to me that everything I built, including my career, was not built on the right foundation. He showed me how I had built so much in my life out of my own strength, such as my marriage or family, and built none of it on Him.

I never started out with a strong foundation. I started with a foundation of wounds, addictions, and unfaithfulness. The house that I tried to build could never stand. When storms came, it would definitely fall. Its end was certain without the right foundation.

God told me that I needed to let go. I needed to let go of finances, worry, fear, guilt, shame, and everything else. I needed to trust that He and He alone would protect me. It went against everything that I always thought about manhood, but now, God told me that was the solution.

"A real man is always strong. He never shows weakness.

If you show weakness, you're no man. A real man protects and provides for his family. A real man takes what he wants and gives others what they deserve. A real man knows how to get a woman into his bed."

I never let go of those teachings. I held to those teachings for years, and now, I could see that it was no foundation for building a life and family. That foundation brought me here.

I never let go of my molestation. I used it to judge how I felt about myself. I never let go of my addictions. I went out of my way to indulge them. I never let go of my insecurities. I still gave power to those old thoughts.

I reached back out to God and said, "God, I surrender to You. Take all of it. Take my past and heal my wounds. Heal my family. Empower me to escape from those addictions. Wash away my guilt and shame. Don't let any of this have a hold over me. Please, Lord, take care of me. I'm Yours."

The decision gave me more freedom than I thought existed. I fell asleep experiencing a complete peace. The driver's seat of my truck felt like a much more comfortable bed than any other. Finally, I didn't stare at the ceiling.

On January 15th, 2018, after washing my face and brushing my teeth inside Walmart, I answered a call from Greg.

He asked, "Ariel, where are you right now?"

I told him the truth. "I, well, I'm at Walmart. I'm living

out of my truck. I lost my apartment."

He didn't even stop to think. "Come stay with us. We have a perfect place for you! It is fully furnished and has all that you'll need."

I didn't answer. My old mindset still wanted to attack.

He said, "I won't take no for an answer. You're coming and we're glad to have you!"

I couldn't hardly believe it. "Thank you, Greg. Thank you so much."

The Holy Spirit prompted him to call me that morning, regardless of my old flaws. More importantly, I wasn't that type of man anymore. I surrendered it all to God. I finally drove to his house and saw his wife, Rhonda, as well as his kids. I didn't know any of them very well.

Greg smiled and said, "We're so glad you're here. Before we show you around, we'd like to take a minute to pray over you."

I don't think they realized that God used them in saving my life that day and the life of my family. I called my daughters and told them, "Girls, guess what? You can come stay with me again!"

The Gunn's often came over and checked on us. I have never known a family as generous, beautiful, and loving as Greg, Rhonda, and all of their children. Over the next six months, I stayed in that little apartment and helped with any project around the house that I could. Greg wouldn't accept any form of rent, so I wanted to do anything to serve this amazing family and pay them back in small ways. Also, I got back into the restaurant business, becoming the general manager at The Shack in OKC.

Things weren't perfect. There were still struggles and hard days, but there were a lot of bright spots. I finally relied on God and not myself.

Lessons Learned

Although it was a miracle that I became a Christian, I had the wrong expectations of Christianity. As you just read, I thought that Jesus could wave a magic wand and make all of my problems go away. I was very wrong.

Don't get me wrong, Jesus works miracles and spares us of many consequences of our sin, the ultimate consequence being Hell and permanent separation from God, but we may still have to experience some of the earthly consequences of our sin in the meantime. My consequences reached a new height at this point in my life, so we have to acknowledge and understand that consequences are real. They demonstrate why we should seek help.

What does God say about consequences?

"Do not be deceived: God cannot be mocked. A man reaps what he sows. Whoever sows to please their flesh, from the flesh will reap destruction; whoever sows to please the Spirit, from the Spirit will reap eternal life." Galatians 6:7-8 (NIV)

This isn't talking about some form of karma. One application of it is simple: If we follow sin and try to please our flesh, we'll experience consequences. However, because we have Christ, there's still that firm hope of eternal life. How do we sow to please the Spirit? That can take a lot of different forms, but I have a few things I want to encourage you to do.

As I mentioned in the last chapter, spend time in God's Word. The Bible will teach you what Jesus wants you to do and how He wants you to live for Him both in your thoughts and actions. We've already been saved by Him and made Him our Lord, so now the Bible helps us to follow Him and know Him better and better.

"All Scripture is God-breathed and is useful for teaching, rebuking, correcting and training in righteousness, so that the servant of God may be thoroughly equipped for every good work." 2 Timothy 3:16-17 (NIV)

God says it better than we can! His Word is useful and prepares us to do good work, so we should read it regularly. Not only that but talking to God is huge. Prayer is powerful and a way to openly express every thought, desire, and request to God.

"And pray in the Spirit on all occasions with all kinds of prayers and requests. With this in mind, be alert and always keep on praying for all the Lord's people." Ephesians 6:18 (NIV)

God doesn't want us to hold back. Take everything to Him and let Him strengthen and grow you through that.

Even when we experience consequences, walking with

Christ will empower us and carry us through any and every situation. We can still have joy and fulfillment as we heal from our wounds and experience freedom from our sins. After trying to find happiness in so many different places, I realized that there is no true happiness or fulfillment without Jesus Christ.

The consequences of sin are endless, ranging from unhappiness, miserable circumstances, suffering, drowning in addictions, and more, but a life-giving, ongoing relationship with Jesus offers us a life full of unconditional love and joy.

CHAPTER 10

But grow in the grace and knowledge of our Lord and
Savior Jesus Christ. To him be glory both now and
forever! Amen.

2 Peter 3:18 (NIV)

What Is the Purpose?

As the divorce moved forward, I decided to have another talk with Camila. Since my perspective changed so much, I wanted to make that clear to her.

I was honest with her and said, "For the sake of our girls, I don't want to fight. You know that I don't want this divorce, but I'll do whatever you want. I want this to be easy and I want us to treat each other with dignity."

Camila replied, "Thank you, Ariel, I appreciate that. Let's just keep doing what's best for Angelina and Julianna."

That became my prayer. As He always does, God answered that prayer in miraculous ways! During the hardest part of the divorce, the girls' school called us and told us how proud they were of Angelina and Julianna. Both were excelling in their classes. They were always kind and offered to help their classmates. The divorce was hard emotionally, but by the grace of God, Camila and I managed to make our daughters the first priority.

Throughout most of the process, I represented myself. Entering court and sorting through everything was an emotionally exhausting process. Again, I relived all of the pain that I put Camila and the girls through. However, God used this process for good by showing me the disastrous effects of sin, unfaithfulness, and divorce.

We finalized our divorce at the end of 2018. I still struggle, but by relying on Christ and His love, I'm getting better. I'm learning to be a better father and I'm learning how to support Camila. We are friends and we try to do the best we can for our girls.

Throughout everything, that same question kept coming back.

"Why?"

Now, I realize that was the wrong question. I never got the answer I wanted because I shouldn't have been asking that question in the first place. There's a different question I should have asked.

"What for?"

Greg told me that there was a purpose to my suffering, and as crazy as it sounded at first, now I know that he was right.

"What is the purpose?"

God always had a purpose for me and for everything that's happened to me. A purpose for everything from the day I was born until now. His purpose was that I would know Him and His Son and experience the unending love they lavish on me. That I would experience His peace when I surrender my brokenness to Him. That I would learn how to fight for my family and teach others to do the same.

Lessons Learned

Finally, I saw the light at the end of the tunnel. I'm not saying that my wounds instantly disappeared. The suicidal thoughts or sexual addictions didn't go away immediately, but little by little, they started leaving. As I've stated earlier in this book, it's a process.

Sometimes, our minds may defeat us in these battles. We'll stumble and fall because we are still imperfect humans. Once again, even after becoming a Christian, we can't fight these wounds and addictions alone. We have to rely on God's grace and mercy.

What does God say about fighting battles?

"You will not have to fight this battle. Take up your positions; stand firm and see the deliverance the LORD will give you, Judah and Jerusalem. Do not be afraid; do not be discouraged. Go out to face them tomorrow, and the LORD will be with you." 2 Chronicles 20:17 (NIV)

God spoke this word to the people of Judah when they assembled before Him to ask for His help against a vast army that prepared to attack Judah and Jerusalem. The people knew they couldn't face them on their own, so they humbled themselves before God, and God miraculously defeated the vast army while the army of Judah simply praised Him!

We may not be in the exact same circumstances as Judah, but the same principles apply in our spiritual battles. God and Jesus deliver us while we stand firm, face our battles, and trust that He is with us. I quoted Ephesians 6 in the last chapter, and now, I'd encourage you to read Ephesians 6:10-18. These verses show that we need to put on the armor of God as we face spiritual battles and that the armor of God enables us to stand against the powers of this dark world and spiritual forces of evil. Even though we may fall, we have a Savior and Lord who overcame sin and continues to empower us to overcome. Take encouragement in that!

Also, there are other practical steps we can take that help us in our battles. First, create new habits to get rid of old, unhealthy habits. If there is a certain routine you have that leads you to succumbing to your temptation, get rid of it and replace it with a new routine! For example, if you usually fall while sitting alone at night, go somewhere else in that time and read the Bible. Call a friend before you go into that situation and ask them to pray for you.

That brings me to the second practical step. Have an accountability partner. I've stated multiple times how important a trusted person is, but this goes beyond simply opening up to that person. Have someone who checks in with you daily or weekly on how you're doing in the battle. Be honest with them and reach out every time you think that there's even the smallest possibility of being tempted.

If we don't take many of these steps, we will be continually discouraged as we fail over and over. Our wounds may still seem inescapable and may dictate our addictions and habits. However, if we really lean on Christ and others, we will see His power and healing at work in all of these areas.

CHAPTER 11

Above all, love each other deeply, because love covers
over a multitude of sins.
1Peter 4:8 (NIV)

Unconditional Love

Now that you've read my story, I'd like to walk you through my journey of what it looks like to fight for your family. However, before I do that, I want to share what I've realized after wrestling with it for years. I recognize now that I didn't know how to love. I struggled with loving myself first, which led to other problems. For example, I didn't know how to ask for forgiveness, which is an act of love. I think this is something we deal with all the time. We struggle understanding and applying love, starting with ourselves.

If you don't have the love of Christ in your heart, it's going to be almost impossible to love yourself or others the way you're supposed to. I'm not talking about just any kind of love. I'm referring to unconditional love, the kind of love that Jesus Christ has for you. He's always with you. He loves you no matter what you do and forgives you every single day. That's the kind of love that I'm talking about. That's what is necessary to fight for your family.

What does God say about unconditional love?

"This is love: not that we loved God, but that he loved us and sent His Son as an atoning sacrifice for our sins. Dear friends, since God so loved us, we also ought to love one another." 1 John 4:10-11 (NIV)

The entire book of 1 John discusses God's unconditional love for us expressed in sending Christ to die for us and how that love plays out in our lives. In fact, verse 16 of the same chapter points out how we "rely on the love God has for us."

Unconditional love isn't natural for us as sinful humans, but in Christ, we find that love for ourselves and as He fills us with that, we can show our family the same love.

I heard over and over that I needed to become the man that God wants me to be for Him, my family, and myself. I didn't have any idea two years ago what that meant, but I do today. I need to be a strong spiritual leader for my family. I need to pray for my family and fight for them through prayer. Over the last two years, I've been becoming that man.

I also need to love Camila as a sister in Christ and my two beautiful daughters unconditionally. We often have conditions, even if we don't realize it. The mindset of, "If you give me this, I'll love you," or, "If you do that, I'll stop loving you," or, "If you hurt me, I'll just walk away." I'm not saying that you should never leave your partner. There are times this needs to happen, especially in the case of abuse. What I am saying, though, is that you shouldn't walk away just because things are difficult.

One of the hardest aspects was getting back my identity as a man and figuring out who I was. Once I did that, I was able to begin healing my heart of all the other wounds from my past, which I've been doing for the last two years. I purposefully made the decision to be the man God wants me. I choose to honor Him with everything in my life, including my sex life. Additionally, I don't want to disappoint Him.

When it comes to my family, I've learned to love them unconditionally. I will fight for my girls. You may ask why I was fighting for Camila for a long time after we separated. I felt that God was leading me to keep fighting for her and not give up. She endured for almost twelve years and waited for me to change. I know she was praying for me to become the man that she had in her dreams. A loving, faithful man, who would love her and protect her forever. I didn't do that. I failed her, but she waited twelve years for me to change before she left. That's why I was waiting on her for that long. I fought for her until God told me to stop fighting for her.

I'm also fighting for my daughters. About a year and a half ago, something hit me. I started picturing Angelina and Juliana marrying someone down the road. I realized that I want them to marry someone like me now, not the Ariel of before. That gives me the courage and motivation to keep working on myself and to become the man and father that God wants me to be for them.

I want to be a good example and role model for my girls. I do this by praying for them in the morning and at night before they go to bed. I also pray for their future husbands. Even simple acts like opening the car door for them or saying please and thank you sets an example. It shows my girls how a gentleman is supposed to act.

Another reason I'm fighting so hard for my girls is because I want to break the curse of divorce in our family. We're carrying several divorces within our immediate family, and I don't want my daughters to ever experience that. Now we're building a new legacy where everyone stays in this loving family. That doesn't mean it's going to be easy and that we won't have problems. We will, but through this journey, I'm teaching my daughters that we fight for what we love, and we love with that unconditional love of Jesus Christ.

Part of that foundation is also showing my girls how to fight for their family and their loved ones in a world that teaches them to move on at the first hint of trouble. The world tells us we deserve better, to be happy, or even to choose whatever is newer and nicer. That may be what we hear all the time, but that's not the answer.

I've met people over the last four years who are on their second or third divorce, and they're still dealing with the same issues. They're unhappy and somehow still connected to their first spouse. Their wounds are eating them alive from the inside out, just like they did to me. Unlike me, they never took the time to heal their heart before moving on.

That is another reason I'm choosing to stay single until God shows me something different. I see people jumping from relationship to relationship looking for something more. If you want more, you need to become more. If you've been doing something for years and don't see the results you want, you have to change. You have to do something different in order to get a different result and fighting for your family is the best "different" thing you can do.

I know all the pain I went through and the pain I caused my family wasn't from God. It was the consequences of my bad actions and poor choices. Again, there was a purpose for it all. The purpose was to lay down the foundation of Christ for all my future generations, to teach them what His unconditional love is, and how to not give up and fight for your family.

I'm standing strong today because my family is worth fighting for. Guess what? If I don't fight for my daughters, nobody will. No one else is going to pray for them or rescue them. That's up to me. I will be able to show them with this book that I'm breaking free from all of my curses. I'm closing the doors on abuse, addiction, and divorce. BROKENNESS stops with me!

As I conclude, I again encourage you to get to know Jesus Christ. Even when I was on top of the world in my career, I never felt happy at work or at home. I only found real salvation in Christ Jesus.

"Salvation is found in no one else, for there is no other name under heaven given to mankind by which we must be saved." Acts 4:12 (NIV)

Give Him a chance. Because of Him I overcame my wounds and addictions. I learned how to be authentic and honest, how to maintain healthy relationships, how to fight for my family, and one of the most important things, how to love unconditionally. I allow Him to continually examine my heart. You can have that same life.

As far as Camila goes, God has showed me very clearly several times in the last year that the door with her is close and it will not open. I am at peace with the door being closed because I did what I needed to do to fight for my family for many years. I do understand it takes two people to reconcile and restore a marriage. That does not mean we can't be reconciled to each other as a Christian brother and sister.

My main role now is to be the example my daughters need. My main goal now is to see Angelina and Juliana follow Jesus and live their lives fully for Him. I trust the Father and I know He has a powerful plan for me and my girls.

For some time now I have been praying for God to show me what to do and how to do it, and most importantly I have been praying for God to honor my heart.

I love you all. God bless you.

Resources that Saved My Life

Family-iD

I would like to talk a little more about Family-iD. Family-iD stands for Intentional Direction and was founded by Greg and Rhonda Gunn about twenty years ago. When Greg first introduced me to it, I was going through the hardest part of my separation. I was hurting and had no direction in my life. As soon as I participated in my first workshop, I started understanding what Family-iD is, what we do, and why we do it.

The goal is to help families align their priorities and begin to set their foundation on Christ. We do this through workshops that focus on teaching how to determine and write out your family vision, mission, and values. Once you do that, we then show you practical ways to live out those statements in order to pass it on to future generations.

We have several formats for the workshop, and the object is for all family members to participate, including children. It's not just about what Mom and Dad want, but what the kids want, too. If they can read and write, they can attend. We want them to have a say in determining their family vision, mission, and values. For all family members, it's extremely empowering.

During the workshop we also talk about relationships. We discuss the needs of a man and the needs of a woman. We go in-depth on how to have a better relationship with your different family members and how everyone in the family needs to treat each other better than best friends. All of these principles put together will help you begin to build a foundation and legacy for generations to come. We don't just leave it at that, either. We follow up with our participants. We want them to start living out what they learned and to start showing the values they chose during the workshop.

Today, Family-iD is in seven countries, and we've impacted thousands of families. A year ago, we were able to take Family-iD to Spanish-speaking families all over the world. We have solid teams in South America. We've trained and developed teams in Argentina, Uruguay, Paraguay, Columbia, and the Dominican Republic. In October of 2019, they led twelve workshops on their own.

The tools learned through our workshops are invaluable to families. Being able to determine your family's vision, mission, and values are vital to its success or failure. Companies, churches, and even large corporations have written mission statements, but I never thought about having the same for my family until I learned about Family-iD.

What does God say about having a vision or making plans?

"The plans of the diligent lead to profit, as surely as haste leads to poverty." Proverbs 21:5 (NIV)

This verse has many applications, but I believe it can also apply to families' plans for themselves. A family will perish without vision and diligence in that vision and in the work it takes. You have to know where you're going and how you're going to get there. If you don't have this, you'll end up in the middle of nowhere without guidance. Family-iD helps give you that direction. It is a compass that will lead you and your family onto the right path.

Family-iD.com

Fight Club

Is men and women fighting for their marriages and families through biblical truth.

Fight Club is a ministry that help men and women to find and obtain a true relationship with God while also helping them to become emotionally stable so they can potentially reconcile with their current or ex-spouse. Being a part of this ministry helps men and women to become the spiritual leader of their family. I started attending the Fight Club Ministry group at the beginning of 2016. During that time, I learned about the emotional wounds I had, and most important, how to heal them. At Fight Club I found honest, authentic, and outstanding Christian men willing to help and support me through my journey. The most important and valuable resource I received from Fight Club was to surround myself with people that would pray with me, hold me accountable, love me, and care for me while I was going through the most difficult season of my life. I would not be here talking to you today if it were not for Fight Club and the men that helped me to grow into the man I am today.

Learn more at Fightclubokc.com

About the Author

Ariel Delgado is of Uruguayan nationality. He is now a citizen of the United States and has made a home for himself in Oklahoma, where he has been for eighteen years. Ariel is and has always been a fighter with a mentality of overcoming any obstacle that comes his way.

He is a life coach, author, corporate chaplain, speaker, and financial advisor. His passion has been developing leaders in the restaurant business, commercial construction and various ministries for the last 10 years.

Ariel is the father of two beautiful young women named Angelina and Juliana, and they are his life purpose. In the last four years he has become a spiritual leader to his daughters, guiding them towards the principles of Jesus Christ. He does not only bring these Christian principles to his family. He is the regional leader in the U.S. and Latin America for Family-iD ministry. Nothing in his life compares to his passion for God and his dedication to help restore families. His vision is to bring a message of family restoration to every corner of the world.